ISBN 978-1-331-91080-0
PIBN 10252866

1 MONTH OF
FREE
READING

at
www.ForgottenBooks.com

By purchasing this book you are eligible for one month membership to ForgottenBooks.com, giving you unlimited access to our entire collection of over 1,000,000 titles via our web site and mobile apps.

To claim your free month visit:
www.forgottenbooks.com/free252866

English
Français
Deutsche
Italiano
Español
Português

www.forgottenbooks.com

Mythology Photography **Fiction**
Fishing Christianity **Art** Cooking
Essays Buddhism Freemasonry
Medicine **Biology** Music **Ancient
Egypt** Evolution Carpentry Physics
Dance Geology **Mathematics** Fitness
Shakespeare **Folklore** Yoga Marketing
Confidence Immortality Biographies
Poetry **Psychology** Witchcraft
Electronics Chemistry History **Law**
Accounting **Philosophy** Anthropology
Alchemy Drama Quantum Mechanics
Atheism Sexual Health **Ancient History**
Entrepreneurship Languages Sport
Paleontology Needlework Islam
Metaphysics Investment Archaeology
Parenting Statistics Criminology
Motivational

NINETY-FIVE

A CALENDAR FOR THE YEAR MDCCCXCV WITH SOME SELECTIONS FROM CANADIAN WRITERS AND DRAWINGS BY MEMBERS OF THE TORONTO ART STUDENTS' LEAGUE

DESIGNED AND PUBLISHED BY THE TORONTO ART STUDENTS' LEAGUE 75 ADELAIDE STREET E. TORONTO
CANADA

THE dry
    dead leaves
      flit by
      with their
          weird tunes,
Like
    failing
      murmurs
        of some
        conquered creed,

Graven
      in
    mystic markings
      with
        strange runes,
That none but stars
    and
      biting winds
        may read.

A. LAMPM

COAL MINERS NOVA SCOTIA

IN reawakened courses
    The brooks rejoiced the land;
We dreamed the Spring's shy forces
    Were gathering close at hand.
The dripping buds were stirred,
    As if the sap had heard
The long desired persuasion
    Of April's soft command.

CHAS. G. D. ROBERTS

To-night
    the west o'erbrims
      with warmest dyes,
Its chalice overflows
    with pools
        of purple
      coloring the skies,
Aflood with gold and rose,
And some hot soul
    seems throbbing
    close to mine,
As sinks the sun
      within
    that world of wine.

I seem to hear
    a bar of music float,
And swoon into the west,
My ear can scarcely catch the whispered note,
    But something in my breast
Blends with that strain, till both accord in one,
As cloud and color blend at set of sun.

E. Pauline Johnson

SUMMER

Quebec! how regally it crowns the height
Like a tanned giant on a solid throne.

CHARLES SANGSTER.

Champlain
Market:
Quebec.

Grand
Battery
Quebec

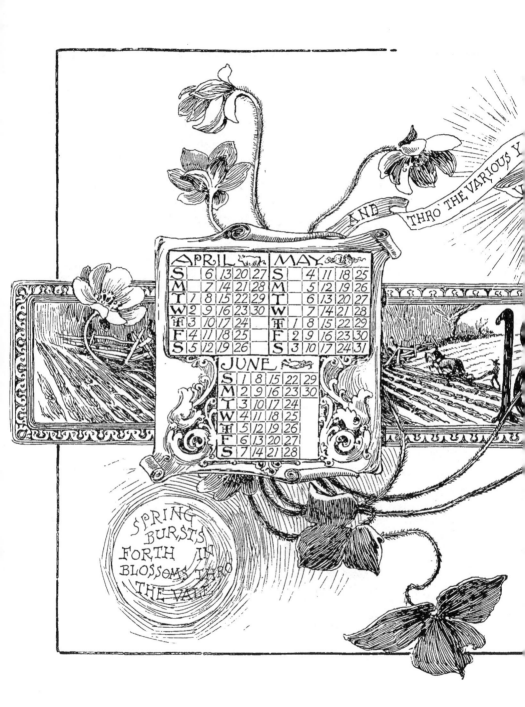

AND THRO' THE VARIOUS Y...

APRIL

S		6	13	20	27
M		7	14	21	28
T	1	8	15	22	29
W	2	9	16	23	30
TH	3	10	17	24	
F	4	11	18	25	
S	5	12	19	26	

MAY

S		4	11	18	25
M		5	12	19	26
T		6	13	20	27
W		7	14	21	28
TH	1	8	15	22	29
F	2	9	16	23	30
S	3	10	17	24	31

JUNE

S	1	8	15	22	29
M	2	9	16	23	30
T	3	10	17	24	
W	4	11	18	25	
TH	5	12	19	26	
F	6	13	20	27	
S	7	14	21	28	

SPRING BURSTS FORTH IN BLOSSOMS THRO' THE VALE

SCENES
...ORY
AND MELT AWAY

JULY
S		6	13	20	27
M		7	14	21	28
T	1	8	15	22	29
W	2	9	16	23	30
TH	3	10	17	24	31
F	4	11	18	25	
S	5	12	19	26	

AUGUST
S		3	10	17	24/31
M		4	11	18	25
T		5	12	19	26
W		6	13	20	27
TH		7	14	21	28
F	1	8	15	22	29
S	2	9	16	23	30

SEPTEMBER
S		7	14	21	28
M	1	8	15	22	29
T	2	9	16	23	30
W	3	10	17	24	
TH	4	11	18	25	
F	5	12	19	26	
S	6	13	20	27	

HOWARD

AND THE
ASTER IN
THE WOOD
IN AUTUMN
BEAUTY STOOD

SING me a song of the toiling bees,
 Of the long flight and the honey won,
Of the white hives ᴜnder the apple trees
 In the hazy sun.

Sing me a song of the thyme and the sage,
 Of sweet marjoram in the garden grey,
Where goes my love Armitage
 Pᴜlling the summer savory.

DUNCAN CAMPBELL SCOTT

Bright were the scenes that fancy drew,
And blithe the hours that gaily flew,
In life's gay morn, when all was new.

CHARLES HEAVYSEGE

'TIS time for vagabonds to make
　　The nearest inn.　Far on I hear
　The voices of the Northern hills
　Gather the vagrants of the year.

BLISS CARMAN

The world is Vagabondia
To him who is a Vagabond

J.M.F.ADAMS

T HEN a light cloud rose up for hardihood,
    Trailing a veil of snow that whirled and broke,
    Blown softly like a shroud of steam or smoke,
Sallied across a knoll where maples stood,
Charged over broken country for a rood,
    Then seeing the night withdrew his force and fled,
    Leaving the ground with snowflakes thinly spread,
And traces of the skirmish in the wood.

DUNCAN CAMPBELL SCOTT

EARLY SNOW!

From the far-off mighty rivers,
Drifting, shifting, glad-life givers,
    Throbbing, pulsing, to the lakes ;
From the far-off, blue-peaked mountains,
From the forest-girdled fountains,
    Where the sunlight leaps and shakes ;
    From the spaces wild and dreary,
    From the cornlands far and near,
    Comes the Autumn's miserere,
    Comes the death-song of the year.

W. W. CAMPBELL